THE WAY HOME

THE WAY HOME

MILLICENT A A GRAHAM

PEEPAL TREE

First published in Great Britain in 2014
Peepal Tree Press Ltd
17 King's Avenue
Leeds LS6 1QS
UK

ISBN 13: 9781845232344

Supported using public funding by
ARTS COUNCIL
ENGLAND

CONTENTS

Walls   7
In Transit 2   8
Inheriting a Stewing Pot   9
Dead   10
"On the Stairway"   11
Christmas Was…   12
News   13
The Way Home   14
The Yard   21
Bird   22
Catadupa   23
Voice after the Tombing   24
Breadfruit Tree   25
In Transit   26
Reading Center   27
Song of the Croaker   28
Sleepless   29
Lobe   30
Poui   31
Mind the Guinep Fly…   32
Autumn   33
Vinyl Rock   34
The Sender   35
A Horse's Lament   36
Ebb   37
Meditation   38
Going Home   39
Prayer for Morning   40
Sting   42
Moon on the Veranda at Bromley   43
Growth   45
Potato Eater   46
Kendal, 1957   47
Somewhere Sunday…   51

Negro Aroused   53
Grief   54
Anchors   55
Dandelion Heads   56

WALLS

More and more the landscape does
not repeat its lignum vitaes.
I recall heads of purple ribbons,
the cursive lingo of furious yellow wings,
the gnawing caterpillar dropping
wood, green, from its yellow jaw,
while an old house bows to a progressive design.

Father grew us accustomed to walls
that pulled in barefoot-boys like sirens' song.
He raised a high chord along the side of
his daughters' lives. It became ritual
for boys to come from all about,
spend whole days, passing
cigarettes – each teaching each to grind
the hand-middle with a blackened nail.

I watched the fog of floating conversations
dilly-dally like the wedded butterflies' script
and lost one brother to the posse's paved climb;
one who loved the greenheart's shade, who ripped
his yellow wing, a father's favourite son,
who abandoned the lignum vitae
for a block some new contractor laid.

My mind, burdened with ribbons, doubted 'til
I unclenched his fist and found
no black stigmata, but red, red eyes,
and the distance mounting walls would bring.

IN TRANSIT 2

The froth-foam on my windscreen disfigures
the burrow of his nose. I wrinkle too
and stiffly oppose his reaching palm
that traded tree-climbing scars and grass cuts
for blades. A brittle boy, his big-man eyes
and big-man ways betrayed by bald underarms.
Lights change and thankfully I pass

the empty parking lots heavy with the ghosts
of concrete nog houses – new tarmac
where porches once fanned ornamental palms.
I strain to hear if night air carries voices:
the sound of women whispering at fences;
of running water, dragon-green, in trenches;
of wheezing youngsters baring chests at scrimmage;

the #35 to Havendale's screeches;
a young girl cutting her eye on a driver's whistle,
and women waiting in and out the bus
shifting weight from leg to leg to ease the hinges
of kneecaps creased like almond bark.

I, too, once knelt on terrazzo, hair in fans,
coconut oil glistening in my palms –
'til horns move me
to smooth out stubborn cracks.

INHERITING A STEWING POT

I point at gossamer silks with golden scales,
window of jewelled shoes and saris that reflects
two women and a girl in pieces.
Above us the sky is inky as night.

Far from the house my belly growls
as we round the rows of halal meat.
Later we throw fallen leaves into the fire;
the flames snatch the ochre fans of the beech

and shrivel them to ash. My mom
and aunt bicker while uncle wets
his crackling lips, and warms my feet.
I don't complain.

Auntie presses her watch into my hand,
embroidered gold, her voice bottomless
from swigging ole Jamaican friends, the damp
coal of her mouth primped to a proper line.

Pepper explodes beneath a maroon lid.
A dutchy would be better, Mother weighs;
the meat seethes, stirring in a metal gut.
I watch the scorch-red flame burn bluer, bluer.

The pot stews; steam pushes at the cover,
weaving silk on kitchen's surfaces.
My uncle peels potatoes, brown as beech,
and sips red fire from a whisky glass.

DEAD

I heard of one, then waited for the names
of two others; they say they come in threes,
you know. At once a sleeve of souls is wreathed,
cut from our lives and soon from memory.

But still a fragrance stirs the air
like passion-fruit vines or stephanotis,
and stems to every trigger in this earth,
starting some swift withdrawal from an inward bank.

They frighten me, these gems deposited
within some casual moment. How can we know
which ones to keep, which ones let go?
And more, once planted, which will grow?

"ON THE STAIRWAY"
for GBW

This is your junction. On one ascent
you showed me the black rock face
you called beautiful; your eyes were bamboo green.
I carry that now, the way men carry God.

I have dug to where your face was strongest
and found ebony strained with orange blossoms,
and the sun, like the wafer in a lizard's throat.
Now, what image scurries up from your chair?

I remember the stairway, you at Goblin Hill,
your top-half eaten by darkness.
The moon dogged your calves as you climbed the mahogany stairs.
You turned to me, your green eyes flickering,
then you were gone.

No more fondly to touch your bare head,
no more spendthrift nights
playing scrabble endlessly on the redbrick patio
while the lights of the men burned below!

Your hair was an ash halo, your graphite lips
were like a child's shading, relentless! Gwyneth,
where are you, gone from the garden?

CHRISTMAS WAS…

… the icy-mint breath you always gave me;
the sermon's dimmed light cowed
to the Christmas star; a sleeved head ascending
the pulpit, as I found sleep in the hollow of your armpit.

It was copper gilding on white coconut flakes –
my burning knuckles, mistaken for raw lumps,
passed too close to a grater's perforations.
I winced and flashed the sting away. I learned

to cook as Beckno told stories of hatpins
his mother used to prod him. Hungry, he spun
the kitchen-bitch till its blunt point landed, then ate
the winnings: veined kidney pegs of tangerine.

These were the things that made a season bright.

Once, in the dark I sat up and stared at the sky,
a whale, captured in a pane of glass, my eyes running
over silver scales. I swore I saw a host
of reindeer pulling you away. Now, outside,

the red kettle has the allure of a browning.
She rings the bell for young men to turn
out their pockets and force the odd bill through
a narrow slit that favours her parted lips.

The good plates and silver do not match;
the domino table is a dusty computer stand;
we make a meal out of few ingredients –
charity and hope – and sleep from feastfulness.

NEWS

I watched their lips and measured how the pair
could move and smile at once, each overlapping,
happy as clams! Only I felt the grain,
something sandish oystering the brain.

They might have spoken, but the rapid lift
of their eyelids is what exchanged the news,
each lash returning the other's blunt stroke –
silence batted away.

Outside, a humming bird was piercing the same flower
and dew was brimming on that flower's leaf.
I felt a taut thread, when all was said,
and withered at what must follow –

the rhetoric of who or what it is
and why this hurt.
A flutter, dew lifts, beak stabs at the familiar.
Tomorrow, this will all happen again.

THE WAY HOME

I

Outside, the plum tree, at a loss
for leaves, lifts at the bull-wind's charge.
Its branches' defiant lances
aim at their grey heaven and toss
relentlessly around the house.
Boughs "x"'; those intersections sing.
In the yard, shades of rain
shrink to a tarnished ring
where, from nothing, the memory comes
scrambling like water.
                    The way home
to small feet is more than one
can sum; a few yards of sidewalk
seems like lots to a child
sprawled in the dust, betrayed
by criss-crossed limbs.

II

Black bumble bees attack
the shower-of-gold. Limp
from sugar, I stagger back –
to Four Square Basic School,
to keloid-bumble bees
that scarred my brother's
naked biceps, who,
hauling, sent me sprawling
on the pavement
to sudden-stinging pain,
the lunch pan spilling its guts, my knees
battered as fallen naseberries.
Small-faced, clouded for rain,

nothing mattered but
my brother's grumbles in the throat
about that fool-child, who could not
master elementary steps.

III

In an empty classroom
I stirred on an iron chair, legs
dangling in eternity; still
I stared at the blackboard's grey
smoke-screen, and reformed
the vanished numbers and vowels
segregated by a white line
as per Britannia's rule.
A big girl came, drowning in a tunic
dark as the sea, and reached
for my brother's geometry set.
I cried when she stole
his rubber heart with its bubblegum smell,
my brand new sharpener with
its shiny blade.
Her shine-eye turned
my dumb suffering to lies.
But I was too small to hang myself
by the neck like the bird mobiles.

IV

And someone just forgot!
So girl, impatient in
a gloomy kindergarten,
with anger's hunger-pang,
retraced morning's steps

without a brother's hand,
or bribery, or edging.
Arms lifted, fright like the
spinning heart that stops
and feels the earth-pull of
its breadfruit weight,
at gully's ledge,
curving, I descended
on paradise plum dare,
the chasm's dirt shoulders
hot and scarleted as my tongue.
Flanked by a schoolbag
to the rusty bridge, to thirty
wooden steps taken like prayers –
the one I knew –
God is good and God is
great let us thank him for our food

V

I raced from twenty-five
to thirty, then breathed
the smell of cut grass and
believed the sidewalk then.
From a pruned hibiscus, a man
handed me blooms and showed
me how to peel blood petals
and wear their pointy-green noses.
He was the stranger they warned
me not to talk to, or take from –
but every day Eve falls
however the voice of God flails.
The dead hibiscus scattered,
trampled on sunless trails,
I heard my father's call

and hid in a space
between lightpost and wall.
My feet in dimpled earth,
I squatted there to wake
the Nanny colonies
sing promise – rice and peas.
Yet nothing surfaced when
I stirred the sand. I found
instead these signs of rain.

VI

I matched the Roman numbers to
the address on an unstamped envelope –
linen white as the hospital sheet.
I, too, was lost, becoming unsealed.
When did the taxi retreat,
when did I stand with tree-strangers,
in a flapping coat?
On this kerb, at this white house, the lace
curtains of the bay window keeping
the darkness inside, here,
where even the colour
of the bricks that made the path-
way had no name,
I sat and wept,
scooped myself to make
a large thing small.

VII

I rested the last container on
the bed and brushed the white
from lips that knew no words,

17

only the salted breath,
and, following his gaze,
I covered loaves of feet,
ignored the curling toes,
small-talked of future walks
that caused his eye to fly
further than soles could bear.
I could not follow where
they stayed and soon I steered
away and wanted home.
I wanted hunger's pang,
the gullies fast with rain
where stony sidewalks ran
and gravel loosely sprang.
I wanted five again,
to carry a child's hate
and not her brother's weight.

VIII

My mother wears the lines
that life has stencilled in
around her eyes. I see
her black pupils in white
holes shrink like a shadow
that suffers in a lit house.
I tense in this old school –
the familiar sounds in her throat
of scattered grains churning
towards a funnel's end,
like greaseless ball-bearings,
or the chafing of crossed limbs
in the plum tree's worn spot.
Her eyes, busy on me,
are disappointed bees;

they do not stop where the
flowers grow bloomlessly.

IX

June starts dry. Mother is a cloud
hesitating across the glass
of the framed photo, where
I imagine her nursing – the dark
blue of her reflection on
a son – pumping an inhaler
with sardine-smelling hands,
to loosen his chest. How weightless,
thrown over her shoulder
like the fallen not left behind!
Then I feel the heaviness
of my own wanting, for her
to lift me from this dust.

X

Most trees have gone;
new strangers spring;
the shade of the old house
drops around my ankles like
a frock. I step out; a wind
flashes like a 'lass and snaps
a breadfruit's stem. I curl
at splattered yellow heart,
at grey-light from shifting leaves,
at things I never loved –
the first few drops that start
a drizzle or my fall.
I load my arms with clothes

that once belonged to loss —
his favourite faded graffiti —
then fast as limbs can carry
I cradle them from rain.
Somewhere inside I feel
this woman knows the way
to gather up the wash,
still damp but mostly quailed.

THE YARD

We lived our lives among things that decayed.
In the yard, the carcasses of deportees
became our refuge when we were afraid.
Inside their rust fatigue is where we'd be,
watching the emerald-dragon dart its tongue
to stab the diamond-back spider that spun
its silver in the hollows of the frame.
We learned the normalcy of death, and shame,
of sitting by powerless – worse – reluctant
to intervene. Trapped in that web we glimpsed
darkness through the bangs of a flapping door,
we felt dread forming from its metaphor
and our hearts grew giant.
How memories seem to jab away at us,
even as we live inside their rust.

BIRD

Caught in peak hour, day ending in a burst
of crimson while a tide of traffic glimmers,
I looked and saw a small thing beating wings
against a tide I cannot feel in this
steel capsule, fogging from cold air,
pressing on, determined to cross the sky!

I cranked the thermostat when he appeared
afraid of an unthawing glacier, that this green
might give him continent to land. My heart
is that migrating bird.

CATADUPA

It's tourist time in Catadupa. Yesterday's air
is sealed in a kindergarten desk. No hand comes
to lift the lid to screw face at cheese-trix crumbs
alive in webs and planets of chewed out bubblegum.
Nothing trickles from the tarnished gold
lip of the standpipe in the raked yard where
the earth has forgotten the hash of soles.
No one is sick today. The chainey root
and raw-moon bush have caused the pot-
water to rise. River cataracts spew as well,
tossing an occasional rosebud-apple.
Here, everyone is gathering wooden birds to sell.
Behind the black huffs of the steamer,
and the charge of that one-eyed bull,
is the pelting song of a Singer
sewing machine, spitting out tracks of new clothes
to barter for a few pound notes.
That was before the '90s, when we measured out
too small a cloth for ourselves, before we sought
new routes, eastward, through the mountain way.
Funny how the school is empty, still;
machines derail and birds decay.

VOICE AFTER THE TOMBING

A blood sun dampens
and a saviour raises

my name, again
my name,

stirs the chalky debris
– Gilbert without winds.

I hallucinate 'lasses
hacking fell limbs.

That sound pierces – still.

I cork ears and dread
hush
over earth's rumble

and a ghost foot's stumble.

BREADFRUIT TREE

Suicidal fruit, abandoning their youth
for the unknown ground and its hush,

leapt happily from her limbs,
severed the navel strings.

Her roots garner strength from their humus
and she sways while the wind hums a chorus.

Who mourns as the earth is digesting?
What coffins roll down to this resting?

She sings sankeys, soft in her leaves,
she bends and she breaks, for she grieves.

IN TRANSIT

A crowd climbs between us
spilling the noise of years. In all
directions I turn to see

you on the faces of strangers (your corm nose
disappears when a man shifts fully into view),
you, by the coffee stand, stirring espresso.

When did your hand slip out of mine?
My palm doesn't burn with your heat any more.
I thought of you, thumb stroking my thumb
till breath stuck in my throat.
I can't believe I lost you.
Never felt you go –

READING CENTER

I went with a novel idea! To read to them
from a shelf where nothing familiar was written
for girls named Crystal and Patience.

I cautioned them, *Sit front and centre*,
thinking these stories could brighten
the angry mouths of their houses.

I thought I would reach
the bleached faces, colour them in.
I never looked beyond the plywood panes

at girls named Crystal and Patience,
pencil thin with resistance for hair,
who pulled at me to part skin-lines,

soothe their damaged roots,
press against their scalps, my palms filled
with enough oil to let life and fate-lines disappear,

to plait new styles, to let
the child-old faces glisten,
for girls like Crystal,

like Patience,
criss-crossed on a balding carpet,
who never listened.

SONG OF THE CROAKER

With sopping, a callus heals and we might climb
out of our skins, like a croaker peeling the
layer to some old hurt,

but softness is not what we choose to be.

The sound growing in the croaker's windpipe
is doubt, is swell and swallow-back;
I look at her, taking slow dragon steps
towards my bed. Too late for panic,

too late for straw broom, a last sweep
by we who cannot not sleep,
but hold moon-bellies and sop and sop.

I dare you come
come sing your song –

The croaker hides from me.

SLEEPLESS

Sometime around one-ish I am made aware
of my own spine's creak, the discomfort of a chair.
Yet — still — white sheets turned down on a divan
spark nil appeal to my fascination
with the grey fresco of a television's rem
and the goosesteps of my obedient thumb,
marching scenes — a window's grainy reflections.
I probe the cut and hardness of a stone
once flung at fruit and fleeing things alike,
child-pebble that seemed large in a lake
but shrunk external to its element,
brought now to light, that some elusive sense
might surface and show why it lies alone,
and why the soft linen, so stiffly drawn,
seems as numbing as the moon's fingertip.
The hour hand moves, eager to progress,
and I fixate on an enduring scene —
a girl of sixteen, perhaps seventeen,
standing on a dirt road, in a yellow dress,
her back to a surrendering sun, the sky cloudless.
Who knew that stone could sink in a space so thirsty?
In this dim room, a girl in her mid-thirties
laps her robe around her hunger and feels
her own clock, the agitated wheels
grinding against the hardness of her seat
as she shrugs off sleep and clutches the remote…

LOBE

The queen conch's lobe pressing the ocean will
someday turn up lost on a sandspit, full
of her memory's echo. I lie awake,
grudgingly dug from sand,
one ear pressed against the night's slab
harbouring house-noises – the pace
of an old clock militant in its rounds;
the croaker mistaken for an insomniac bird;
the flap-flap-flap of a list of "things to do",
impatient though the world is bedded down,
and the three-blade fan raging on.
Further away a child sobs over
a dream broken by a grown-up's assault,
head full of shards that she may never mend.

These sounds fill the cavity and keep
rest at bay
            for women who pull covers to their chins
and listen for movements radial to the Main.
Not for them splay of the night-surf's slap,
cajoled by the piping rhythm of
a soundboy, selector in the distant Gap
lulling the street, muting the grins of harder shells
'til night's drunk shadows hug a speaker-box.

House heavy with this air
is a place to outgrow.
Carry me then on an island's pulse
to surface on a spit somewhere.

POUI

Your palm slides into mine — soft. Without flinching
you ask, *Lead me to the avenue*
where poui trees spread wide canopies,
your eyes catatonic, ridden by leaves
that form like gilding on vaulted memories.
Give me that city street. Give me a dream
where poui light scathes buildings as they scrape
the belly of a sky too big, too blue,
and sweep the poui cabs that litter the avenue
where women brush their almost poui hair
from poui skin and poui-scented napes.
But all I see is a wire-fan rake,
know the sallow earth's clumping while the moon
in my hand rises on the grate
of a wooden handle. Away
life scuttles! Wind at your brow, you suckle
childhood, reluctant to fall from its stem. Cold
knuckles unclasp a coat's hard buckle. You loosen
the years and years of bellies bursting blue
and gold fandangles that dress the branching families
left here to rake the rotting poui leaves.

MIND THE GUINEP FLY...

De next-door-neighbour's tree
hangs over blanched zinc, and
panicles of ovoid fruit motion
to me. In no time I climb
the rubble of the storeroom,
shifting loose stone
on a collector's tomb
to return, carrying stems.
Minding stain I lean
forward to burst skin...

Even at thirty-six I still heed
the boys' them warning: *Crack
the guinep seed!* And soon,
all jelly peeled,
I tease out the bald nut —
time spent deferring
life's acidic shot.

Once, a fragment flew down
my throat and as I sputtered,
eyes popping, had the wide thought
that a tree's revenge was overdue
around me, the branches banded,

'til finally I spat
that tang of flesh and stain
and feared that years of prowess
and caution were in vain:
the broken skin, the crushed seed
the trees that never came.

AUTUMN

Give me another day of crisp yellow leaves,
of almonds balding shamelessly in spring.
I will not scold my feet's shuffle to
the accidental ring of the
dumb phone on a shiny cradle.
I will not wilt at the sight of sundown.

VINYL ROCK

Show me again
that version of you
fanning a coal pot,
flour-white, crusted hands.
Next thing I know
a small damp pops
and, no surprise,
borne embers scat
like dizzy gingi-flies.

I watch you kneading
through the meshing
that makes my window
a scaled eye.
Your whitish finger
stabs izims at God.
Waistline dip. Dip-

in here, I stay close
to the vinyl's rock,
needle knowing groove.
I twirl in my seat,
plan to feel-out old keys,
first in the mind,
then on a "qwerty" board,
testing the direction
thought-bugs could fly

Instead I scratch,
and keep on returning
to the moment's burning.

THE SENDER

I send message after message, and with each click
a small envelope gathers wings and streaks
into an electric ether – nothing returns;
I imagine pigeons' amputated feet.

Free me from duty that I did not choose.
I was content to coo in a crowded cage
and bury my beak in my own pit for heat.

Another night, another push, as if a weight
slips from one saucer to the other's sentence
and always, when dawn scouts the perimeter,
my blind fingers find what I think are the right keys

…and a bird bludgeons itself against a windowpane
then lies undone by its own reflection. Yet,
heart pounds; heart swells; heart beats again –

A HORSE'S LAMENT

In the dim, I study a mountain's form
and nod its meter as its cardiogram
echoes from Stony Hill to Boscobel.
I keep vigil, believing dawn
and that language of ours – curled fists and tightened knees
when we speed away and know lines like the one
the wind piles in our ears and flings at your sore lips.

Horse without rider is beast!
My heart, saddled, ridden thing,
whinnies in its dread stable and asks:
When will the rooster clear his throat and scratch that sun
from its hole and sun sup night off the cold roof?

When will the watchful chattels squint from light, and figure
limbs to glowing filament? When will darkness move out of our way
and show your hand, cupped, sweet lump, rose-apple?

I straddle a moment that has no sound,
of pupils, startled, shuffling in
sockets that fix upon
once knowing flesh, cajoling rider's bone.

A smudge of breath, closely a second smudge,
then slip – my stirrup separated from sole.
The mountain moved. I heard no thud. Life kept on reeling, and
ear, accustomed to its spooling film, was not prepared
for the swish at the end,

or for night on the ground again, spreading fast as if spilt,
or for strange sounds – the foreign tongue of a boot
striking springless earth;
the pellets' measure rattling the trough;
the loosening of the girth.

EBB

You smiled and waded out beyond the light-
green bands, into the dark water, my mind
buoyed by your reassuring words;
it was your swaying smile I did not trust,

that made my heart a starfish in my chest
or some white fossil, dumb. Beyond the surf
the scream I felt was tangled in the weeds;
it drifted to the oaring of your hands.

Was it my tears turned you back to sand?
I could be brave today, but tomorrow
the bed-sheets will smell of a different sea,
the tide leave a different jetsam.

MEDITATION

Breath after breath, it all crumbles away
as if air is a muted wave loosening
clay from the crimped toes of an old vessel.
Grain follows grain. The days are lost until
a stub too small to hold is all that peeks
from where it lies broken, buried in red dirt.
Will some hand come to form this thing again,
and this time will it be fired in a kiln?
I suck the glaze from my lower lip
and weigh the sun as it bakes me to stone.
A lotus empties pollen in the wind;
I clasp my palms to keep from floating off.

GOING HOME

— for Cooper

As men slam shut the market gate,
my goats whine for the old estate.
The sun slipped from the sky so fast
I never saw them separate!

The trucks pack up each soul at last;
a few walk on ahead. They cast
their shadows on the lucid street;
I watch them move through ginger grass.

No one has stopped for me as yet;
the goats want nothing else to eat,
so I just catch my breath; I know
that dark is curling round my feet.

No shortcut through the ginger row —
my zinc house is *jus a stone-throw*.
I'll soon untie the rope and go
I'll soon untie the rope and go.

PRAYER FOR MORNING

The moon is rising on the hill's back;
my *madda* is not home as yet,
and in the corners, inky and black,
the daddy-long-legs plot and plait.

The candles dart their tongues like spears,
and light that ought to lick out fears
instead climbs curtains, clambers chairs
to start a burning spring of tears.

We clasp our hands, we say our prayer –
Please let the morning find us here.

Outside, lizards *kibber* their sounds
and crickets trade-in violins
for thunderclaps and silvery live rounds,
while daddy-long-legs weave their homes.

An ole dog pokes his nose and barks,
piercing my ear, scratching his mark.
Holes in the walls, holes is the heart!
The moon is cold, the lanes are dark.

We clasp our hands, we say our prayer –
Please let the morning find us here.

Lock up the louvre, latch the grill gate,
out every candle that might light
the corners where daddy-long-legs wait.
Only *Madda* must know this hiding place.

The outside shadows secrets keep,
so mind the door, and fight off sleep;
the moon's face holds – breath taken deep,
'fraid for the daddy-long-legs creep.

So clasp your hands, and say your prayer:
Please let the morning find you here.

STING

for Howard

This time the phone's buzz will not flutter my
girl-heart. I have turned into stone.

I will not be swallowed, though
your hello is as threatening as a storm.

Mommy and I watch, stock sardines and kerosene,
make the most of days, living in the eye.

Remember the roof you nailed to keep us dry?
No damage you did not try to repair.

Often, she talks as if you were still that little boy,
her delight to swab and drain wounds clean,

but then, the boy turn seventeen and raise Cain.
Today she flinches at a pebble's zing,

as you flinched once, let loose from the railings
a shirt, sprawled by a gust of wings. The body quails

to see her will give way to reclaiming grass.
An opener drops on the counter. Hollow sound

of hand drawn quickly from a bitter tin.
She grimaced, I grimaced at the accidental sin,

at the one bleeding she hoped might heal with time.
I will rest the receiver on its cradle, gentle,

heavy with questions and the bee of remorse
that any womb could render such a wound.

MOON ON THE VERANDA AT BROMLEY

She told me once about the knots they tied,
a couple on the veranda. Still the sun
ran out half bleeding and the full moon stayed
tied to the meadow and the cows.

She blamed the land; it willed them to ignite.
The hillside crackled, and words prickled
like patches of crab-grass. We were burning

to watch ginger in the wood's eye
and shadows bend in the mahogany arm
that held the manor house, black as an elbow
sweetly daubed in coconut oil.

She stayed, she and I rapt. The trees'
dark antlers gashed and bucked
as wind grew tall, and dragged the black cloud close,
reeled it in, a tyre on a line.

The end of a cigarette diminishing
into the ruck of her lips, she breathed
a bevy of billowing strands;
the glass of copper smouldered in her hands

and she looked blue, as if the blaze
inside her charred the sides of the wood.
Her bare legs, weighted down in copper, could
not lead her into water, though she hissed.

"You know this fire",
a titter, and I glimpsed
the storeroom in her eyes, her tongue
an ember, cooled to ash.
I saw the pupils leading flames to me.

Eventually, I gave up watching
to dream her, clasped by her own white arms,
her tinted curls caught in the light,
the inside of her thighs melting, a whiff
of hair and wax, the sound of fat's remorse,
of meadow's coal, the cows run into ash.

GROWTH

Something grows by the Seville orange tree –
planted from an old yam head.
It has been sleeping underneath earth's bed,
now it creeps on ground without a stake.

How long since we dug that hole,
roasted and ate our fill of the food?
Towers have burned, our hearts cooled
and the wound long overgrown.

Now this bark is trellis for the plants'
tethering, a new feral vine
that barely hides the crooked K heart M;
sugar beads a scar I long forgot.

Can sweet come from dormant root?
It swells now in the damp, it promises.
If it ripens, will we have nerve to dig?
It climbs to die… I know its leafless sprig…

POTATO EATER

At supper, you reached for my bowl;
the light from the kerosene lamp stirred
on your soft palm.

Your eyes made everywhere
seem harder than earth, or the potatoes
that we dug from the black and damp ground,

and life was simple as this food placed on a table.

KENDAL, 1957

Petty-thief

The train pushes me through the dark landscape,
relentless bull; I am its only horn,
drawn like the switch-blade I done use to scrape
the waxing cheek of a woman. The red scorn
of her lips parted – two accuseful lines
that never trembled even as I pressed,
and droplets, plentiful with star-designs,
made small patterns round the indented crest.
Then I felt like a flying fist, and God
could not stop me. I took her, took her world,
snatched it yellow from its dangling pod
and planted it in my pocket. Now hurled
through the dark by the iron bull I've freed,
my steam billows away, a grey stampede.

Choir

The steam billows away, a grey stampede
retreats to Mo-bay. In the car a crowd
sings alleluia, their pulses gathering speed,
charging to some crescendo. The women's loud
contraltos and sopranos cut night like steel,
and men's baritones level to a moan.
What height kept in this sudden flight should seal
the fates of greater and lesser mortals, thrown
into agony by some passing hand that spills
something precious on a more precious cloth?
In one moment, a silent chasm feels
loss – white and uncertain as a wobbly tooth.
Then, in darkness, some surviving voice hails:
Kendal! Waking us in our sleeping homes.

47

Reggae for Lee Scratch Perry

Kendal wakes me from sleep. Waxing halls
sing spa-na-nap. I write their music, drowned
in the hum of negro spirituals,
with a drop-steady beat. I mix it down,
then roll it; in a field of yellow fever-
grass I chug it, my mouth rounding the smoke.
The cool breeze takes your baby's cries and weaves
them into one endless track. Once I woke
from man-dreams, a twisted caterpillar,
the spa-nap derailed, the notes flung like limbs.
I smelled a tang like the coffee liquor
you get at the end of the railroad lines,
a thing too thick to sample, a wax note
with a feeling like smoke scratching the throat.

Reaper

A feeling comes like smoke scratching the throat;
without eyes, without sound it comes, the knowing
as true as the black reel that guides my iron vessel.
Something is there standing in the glow
the headlights throw. A woman's shadow.
A thousand voices call to me from behind
her. Bare faces embroidered in the folds
of her surging shroud. But where is that wind?
Gone from my lips as soon as I could grasp
the handle of a chain and yank it thrice.
Three blasts it took before my fingers' clasp
fell loose and loosened something else – a stem
of rice, grains rattling in their coat.
She cuts and binds the sheaves, she gathers them.

One Left Behind

I cut and bind the sheaves then gather them
before the dusk falls. I look for the path
my footprints made in the early morning
where the crabgrass refused to sprout new growth.
Something about retracing those steps makes
my mind journey to another home. There,
Capt'n wraps hard-dough bread in foil to take
as lunch for his church convention. Up here
the track is not a discernible line,
only a train, stretched like a segmented thought,
shows where it lies and how the passage winds
then breaks apart. My poor Capt'n, he sought
that path through dark lands alone. He will come
before the moon, and I find the way home.

Waiting at the station

That night the moon and I found the railway
station quiet. Eyes white against the dark
tunnel that bore down on figures who paced
the platform, hunched, leaning toward its arch.
Shoe heels hit boards like the hammering heart,
its pendulum reduced to a metal gong.
Those who came together, now stood apart,
minding wristwatches, their hands twisting on.
Then the blast of a truck horn gave us hope
for one minute; we swore we saw a light
flood the tunnel. We clung to memories' rope
but past reunion ghosts faded from sight.
Then was the allegro of human promise gone,
leaving shadows jumbled in the station.

Porters

They watched shadows, jumbled in the station,
shuffling on the dimly lit ceiling,
glad for the delay, the relaxation
of a domino game. Four, lofty from stealing
time, chug cigars and slap the ivory bones
upon a table balanced on their knees.
Six love! one shouts and calls the game as done;
the three expose their hands and their last piece
falls. Wrapped in this game they tally up score.
The clock gongs two, a fleeting glance is all
they show. Shuffling scattered bones once more
their game resumes and plays into an "L".
Red caps in place, four fritter time till they
must bear the burdens of arriving souls away.

SOMEWHERE SUNDAY…

I

Men pull on white trousers and leave
their beds lingering in lost innings,
while the hats of lovers tilt for a prayer
to tighten love's knees, and love's resolve.

The pitch loosens its moisture;
shirts come undone; creased bibles
bare flesh and ribbing and the sun
on the rooftop of the pavilion

plays noon-light like a three-card man
on the eyes of a bowler who
is swinging his judgement arm
on a nerve and a naked stump.

II

A pressure cooker's whistle drowns
in a loud kiss-teeth; a pudding pan
piles its lumpy batter till
the dents are scrape-finger-clean;

the smell of seasoned coconut-
milk drowns the nostrils, and river
babies and moonshine darlings cup
themselves before jumping, and cannonball

sound smashes, then splutters up water. Careless
laughter is burbling in the surge.
The trees grater noon light, and throw
its powder on turned-up faces.

II

The women are striking the hide
of black bibles; their faces turned up
are gasping swimmers that surface
then dip, then surface again…

The old men rattle teeth and cough
from the striking on their backs, from being
loved too tightly. The way home is a woman
striking asphalt with black spike-heels,

ignoring the noon light's threat to make-up,
the itch of nylon stockings, with a paper
napkin, crushed into a ball, batted
across her blazing temples.

NEGRO AROUSED

Behind you the sea's ankle; land is its shackle
where half-naked you alone search heaven
for death. You find it flapping in pail with tackle,
or smell it on a hand that wrings a slimy chamois,
then passes you a lift. Life, the sting at your eye,
the briny taste – airborne and cruel on the skin –
made you lose sight of me struggling
to pull a snapper from the grit-grey
harbour; two flutter and gasp for breath –
one with nylon lines reddening his hand-middle,
the other's eye cloudy from battle.

GRIEF

For Clyde

What earth devours remains moist in the mind
though the throat itches and the heart retracts;
we cannot help but return, plain as a ghost,
slipping through the door at your back.

ANCHORS

My hand reaches out, touches the lapel
of your coat, hanging from a nail for days,
and, two-twos, before the room caves with the smells
of shoe polish and aftershave, I dip

into familiar pockets and feel the remains
of a crumpled napkin bearing a meal's stains,
and a coin – old delighter that quietly flips
to exchange its tender for a cold flat weight.

Turned inside out and emptied of these anchors,
my white palm flags, then surfaces to routine,
as if tooth did not tear this stone, and more,
some will give way that held these lasting bits.

DANDELION HEADS

Out loud, a floating sentiment
like dandelion heads, I press my lips
to fingertips, then blow you away,
away, a floating dandelion head.
We watch the smallness of befuddled words
and wonder where they go,
slave cargo transported in my bosom's hull.
When did we trade them and for what?
These days gambolled, bodies mused and mislaid,
till who can tell which limbs belong to whom?
Only the whites of their eyes are paired,
rolling in sockets, blank dice perpetually thrown.
How have we beheld these un-sures alone?
Once in the jaw of a wordless night, we steered
our hands toward each other, Calabash Bay
kneading the splinters of shells into stars.
Perhaps God blowing dandelion heads
gave me the falling will to jump at more.
And yet calendar leaves have autumn too,
and through their seasons consciously renew
the thought of you, the promise we will write.
But when? To find words, begin again?
I wonder, while silence worms you away,
will love unravel, pulled too hard, too often?
I feel a sway, as after wine sipped too fast;
my dandelion head floats out of the past
and tugs on my promise's thin string,
anchored to a sentimental phrase.
Let us wait for the fragile thing to break
and ponder where the bay's wind might take
two misguided parachutes who dared
to lunge into the desperate grey.
                    Away Away.
We land somewhere in the cracks
that dandelions know.

ABOUT THE AUTHOR

Millicent A. A. Graham was born 1974 and lives in Kingston, Jamaica where she practices Informatics with an MSc in Human Centred Computer Systems from the University of Sussex. Her interest in poetry began in childhood, rummaging through the family bookshelf where she found Keats, Dickinson and other classic works. She pursued this interest through local societies and later became a member of the Wayne Brown Writers Workshop where she continues to develop her voice and style. Also a beneficiary of the Calabash Writer's Workshop Fellowship, her connection with the Calabash International Literary Festival Trust has exposed her to contemporary writers and new ways of approaching the page. Through these valuable influences She has won local awards for her poetry including the well-established Observer Literary Award for Poetry in 2005 and silver and bronze in the Jamaica Cultural Development Commission (JCDC) Literary Arts Competition in 2005 & 2007. Her work has been published in the anthology *Bearing Witness 3* and *The Caribbean Writer*, Vol 17. Her first collection, *The Damp in Things*, was published by Peepal Tree in 2009.

ALSO BY MILLICENT GRAHAM

The Damp in Things
ISBN: 9781845230838; pp. 58; pub. 2009; £7.99

These poems by Millicent Graham have a compactness and economy that belies the complex and expansive range of emotions and considerations that occupy her imagination. Graham's poems offer us a way to see her distinctly contemporary and urban Jamaica through the slant eye of a surrealist, one willing to see the absurdities and contradictions inherent in the society that preoccupies her. These are poems about family, about love, about spirituality, about fear and mostly about desire, where the dampness of things is as much about the humid sensuality of this woman's island, as it is about her constant belief in fecundity, fertility and the unruliness of the imagination. For a poet publishing her first collection, Graham's sense of irony, and instinct for surprise and freshness in image are remarkably mature and sophisticated. But it is the sharpness of image and the precision in her use of language that announce the arrival of an extremely talented poet: " I am the curve set straight/ by a guava switch, the proof/ that love can make you flinch." Graham knows the tradition of Caribbean poetry, and is deeply aware of the value of both homage and resistance. The result is a wonderfully executed balancing act that ultimately suggests a newness of sensibility and imagination.

In *The Damp in Things*, we are invited into the unique imagination of Millicent Graham, and we find ourselves in a world of psychological density and liveliness, and a space of sharply honed intelligence that remains strangely light and alert because of her slanting wit and off-kilter humour.